MARBLED IN FOAM

MARBLED IN FOAM

CLARE BRANT

All rights reserved. No part of this work covered by the copyright herein may be reproduced or used in any means – graphic, electronic, or mechanical, including copying, recording, taping, or information storage and retrieval systems – without written permission of the publisher.

Printed by imprintdigital
Upton Pyne, Exeter
www.digital.imprint.co.uk

Typesetting and cover design by The Book Typesetters
hello@thebooktypesetters.com
07422 598 168
www.thebooktypesetters.com

Published by Shoestring Press
19 Devonshire Avenue, Beeston, Nottingham, NG9 1BS
(0115) 925 1827
www.shoestringpress.co.uk

First published 2023
© Copyright: Clare Brant
© Cover painting: Ebru in acrylic, by Dmytro Buianskyi

The moral right of the author has been asserted.

ISBN 978-1-915553-37-9

ACKNOWLEDGEMENTS

Shoestring Press says on its website – http://www.shoestringpress.co.uk/ – they specialise in publishing poetry sequences and collections by 'Established but unfashionable poets'. What John Lucas, its founder and energetic editor, does not say is that for unfashionable poets, getting established is a process enabled by him in ways to which it is hard to do full justice. He gives you room to grow. I thank him for his ready support, his wise judgement and his generous editing. I thank Ruth O'Callaghan, a most established poet, for her steadfast encouragement, excellent suggestions and kind friendship. Commissions from Nicola Watson for her project *Romantic Europe Virtual Exhibition* (RÊVE, online at http://www.euroromanticism.org/virtual-exhibition/) helped establish me in a lively and humane literary community. Alan Marshall thoughtfully pointed me to Lorine Niedecker.

For sharing poetry and much else, deep thanks to Katherine Armstrong, Eric Larson, Bridget Lubbock, Jacqui Mansfield, Jim Noble, Sarah Spiller, James Waterfield, Helena Webb, Veronica West-Harling, Roger Whitney. Special thanks to Teresa Brus, for brilliantly translating some of my poems into Polish, and to Claire Cox, for animating and inspiring exchanges. I am grateful to my brother and sister-in-law, Chris and Sarah Brant, for all their support.

To Richard, with my love

CONTENTS

Again the Boy	1
Air Frost	3
Algerian Rock Art	4
Apples	5
Aspiration in the Poetry Room	6
Beetle ID	7
Besides the Weeds and Litter	9
Blinding Truth	10
Blockbuster	11
Body After Body	12
Built-in GPS in Birds, but How?	13
Calm Decay	15
Carotene	16
Cashmere with Holes	17
Cavalier Portrait	18
Cell	19
Coronation: A Commentary	20
Coxitations	24
Death like Love Can Be Ambiguous	25
Desert Flower	26
Disputed Election Results	27
Dulas Brook, Golden Valley, Herefordshire	28
Eden Tree	32
Elephant in the Room	33
Elephantine	34
Explosive	35
Fern	36
Floor Cleaner	37
For Now the Trees	38
Fragments of A History in A Dream	39
Hanging Scroll	45
History Inside Out	46
Impromptu	47

Intimates Down Under	49
Irinya, Katya, Vera…	51
Jamjar Nasturtiums	53
Keep the Art Books	54
Lever Box	55
Marbled in Foam	58
Medellin Hippos	59
Mimesis	60
Moving In	62
My Friend Shirley Says She Will Pray for Rainbow	63
New Year's Eve	64
Nocturnal Jasmine	65
North Lincolnshire	66
Now We Are Sixty	68
Rainbow Fades…	69
Rainwatching	70
Reflection	71
Remember the Alamo	72
Rereading 'The Walrus and the Carpenter'	74
Sea Shanty for the Cows in a Floating Farm, the Netherlands	75
She and He	76
Skip	77
Slow-Worm	78
The Eel Question	79
The Poet's Dog's Complaint	80
The River at Port Meadow	81
Thinking of Alfred Cohen	83
Time Scales	84
Today	86
Tribute	87
Was It Better than Suburbia?	88
Watlington	89
Wayfarer	90
Wishbone	91

AGAIN THE BOY
After seeing Franz Lenbach's painting, 'Shepherd Boy' (1859).

Again the boy, lying sleepily on grass
one arm shading his eyes against the sun
one knee bent, lolling

I return to him
all the love I did not have
condensed to butterfly, hovering

disturbing the drowsy light, blue ocean
youthful dream

a flight of whit buttarflyes so high and thick
you could not see the town of Calleys

this in July, 1508
take it on trust

palsy, shakes, determination
to shake off shake and palsies

mind over matter
does not always work

I and the apple tree interwoven
fruiting, laden, felled
by its own weight

obliteration of oblivion
cast in fertility of pips
in an apple, a question, temptation

particular pale pink of apple blossom
and the sparrows hopping in its branches
purposive, concealed

what is it all for, asked a friend
the coupling, the children, the home making

or the boy, again the boy, on a hot summer's day
lazing away metaphysics.

AIR FROST

Spooked trees
held fast to all they knew
the woods were fairycastle ogreish

ice whitening every bracken frond
began to drip translucent time
and glacial secrets

we were lost
in a copse of branching paths
when suddenly sun shone through

frosted air
bewildered wildness lessened
we found our way.

ALGERIAN ROCK ART

Slender elegant figures
appear on the walls
in black and white
tremulous stone

older than the pyramids
antelope   crocodile
geometric hunting
horses mid-gallop

horned, dotted, fringed
our ancestors
their anklets jingling
dance across the walls of time.

APPLES

Apples in fairy-tale red among the changing greens
warn of ambition, appetite and the anxiety we
never quite lose about whether
good things are dangerous
or bad things fatal

so they dangle, akin to equilibrium
whether this apple is best for a pie or sauce
or biting almost to the core of juiciness
whether the leaves surrounding say
it's better to leave in a scarlet blaze
or return in green

the terminal bud has done its job
it toileth not, and yet
what effort to make an apple
swell with such import
its fairy-tale red blocks out the changing greens.

ASPIRATION IN THE POETRY ROOM

'An elaborate mirror hangs next to the entrance to the Poetry Room...'
Library of Congress, about its Poetry Room.

You bet it does
mirror mirror on the wall
it has gold ornaments
'(mirror glass is slightly compromised)'
birds beat upward
straining to the heavens
whose emblem is pagoda

I wish to unclutter the background
from reflections
so that my self is framed
simply in elaborations

it is a start

was I announced?
Who makes my claims
but I
who does not know
unwoven rainbow

I am untitled
unentitled maybe
in unvoluminous dress
looking at, not out
not looking in
pretensions surround me
I am all surface
and surfacing from depths.

BEETLE ID

Corydalidae
corry dally dye
there are 63,000 species of rove beetle
is this one

what's in a name
what does it matter
exactitude
in the absence of infinitude
every meeting matters
however chance or fleeting

brown wing case
elytra
beetle-unique forewings on the second thoracic segment
wing protectors
two red spots
gold-ringed tapered body
six legs and what seem to be mandibles

leaf-crunching language
it is hard to learn

perhaps the beetling insect
emergent in sun
has to learn flowers, plants, predators
greens, shadows, weather

beetle life, my life, intersect
whatever the genus or species
we are family

the human looking at me
has camera lens and spectacles
righteous looming
fascination with labels

and dedicated to presenting
how summer morning
uplifts us both.

BESIDES THE WEEDS AND LITTER

We pass a cherry tree where dogs' pee
has burnt away the bark

the clouds, small cumulus
gather heavier grey

like cirrus floating down
little weights mass

wheelchair dahlia war data theft
space junk

my head's in the clouds so I do not see
something wince as my dog squirts on the cherry tree.

BLINDING TRUTH

Ophthalmologists have warned against the use of shotgun 'birdshots' by security forces who have blinded over five hundred protesters in the Islamic Republic of Iran.

The things her eyes had learned to see
beginning with her mother's face
her father sisters brother
a tree
of pomegranates

through open door of home
a window out
carefree clouds
darkening
to no door out

no turquoise scarlet purple
no orange
except in oranges
she laid their peel against her skin

she dreamed in yellow
green
envied the rose
pitied herself

even as her bandaged eyes wept
she saw herself
brave
proud
a figure for truth, blinded.

BLOCKBUSTER

That Daddy who happens to be President
is much too close with his daughter
she's too bound up in him
where's Mom?

Here comes arachnid Mother
swinging down on us with menace
whip-smart, her will to dominate
is all-devouring

her minions attack the fleet
stuff explodes
who is loser who is victor
terabytes of starburst tell us

maverick scientist with girlfriend
(who is allowed to know a thing or two)
devises a plan
a scene the writers sweated over
bomb Mother, obviously

shiny, slimy, insectoid, ultramachine
no wonder we don't love Mother.

BODY AFTER BODY

Death isn't fussy here
basic respect will do.

Here they come, masked
body after body
after body after body
after body after body after body

stretching to a bleak horizon
familiar, unexpected history

a grey of storms and graves
dead albatross litter the decks
shrouds, guns, hashtags, lamentations.

What must we do?

BUILT-IN GPS IN BIRDS, BUT HOW?

Flying high above a hot and glittering city
there is one building to avoid, say
the pigeons whose ancestral range
overlaps with glass and concrete city.
Beware a laboratory, in a medical school
both prestigious and cheap.

These qualities are relative
especially to pigeons
whose excellent navigational skills
became interesting to professors
in a laboratory dedicated to brains.
Bird brains are similar to humans, they said
so they trapped some pigeons and put each in a box
magnetised on each side. Now show us, they said
what you are made of –
whether it is your hippocampus or your inner ear
that hides your receptors
or is it your beaks?
Let us damage each part in turn
and see what lights up
when we magnetise the box.

The results, sadly, were not conclusive
a firm conclusion was elusive
nonetheless, it was professed
that pigeons' vestibular nuclei did respond
to changes in the magnetic field
in ways that might have a bearing
on how humans make their spatial maps.

Some cells were sensitive, said the report
whose publication increased the prestige
of the college in the glittering city
below the pigeons flying in tune with the Earth
between the desert and the sea.

CALM DECAY

In ruined colours the tulips
gesture to tapestry
loosely

they reach out to extend
their being
their temporary knowledge of existence

crumpling silks of pale yellow
ghostly amethyst
painstaking scarlet curls

coming undone
arching open
bent as if windblown

a breath of air will destroy
their calm decay
leave them undisturbed for one more day.

CAROTENE

I am supposed to be cooking something
new recipe is ready
it says carrots
carrots, slim and young

o forget any thought of dinner
let us consort, cavort with carrots

laze in a yacht off Capri
dance till the sun says good morning, good morning
see in the dark all that slim and young
can touch and taste and smell
hearing in carrot teen a whoosh of slim and young

which is immortal
thunderous
delicate

I have forgotten what I might be making
except it involves carrots, young and slim.

CASHMERE WITH HOLES

The last time you bought one you bought two
thinking when one wears out
there'll be another one

if only we could do that
in other dealings
another set of threadbare wouldn't matter

instead I sort and size up
what's mendable and what's to be cast off.

CAVALIER PORTRAIT
Ritratto di cavaliere dell'ordine constantiniano, Vittore Ghislandi (1655–1743), Museo Poldi Pezzoli, Milan

The face is so small a part of him
squeezed by a tight-curled wig and heavy hat
felt welded, pinched, coaxed to curve, pinned
above rich grey-green coat

his mouth full and plummy
like his voice

dangling gold-handled cane
a carefully careless sash

there is blackness behind him
all the light is sucked into silvering
the bold broad edging of his jacket
he's wealthy, but he wants something from you

it's blindingly obvious
the man knows a good tailor

his military bling self-decorative
he's armoured now in lace

the painter used his fingers, not a brush
underneath his edgy strokes, a man
to whom appearances will always matter
appears as if, mysteriously, appearance did not matter.

CELL

The humans are not coming out
of their houses, their shacks, their holes in the ground.

Someone caught and someone bought a bat.
The bat bit back, hitting bloodstream.
A virus jumped host and dug in.

Millions of humans got sick.
A million or two or three
four five six more than six million so far have died.

The humans are not coming out
afraid of being sick
I am not coming out
I am sorry I ate that bat
I am sorry I ate the forest
I would put things back.

CORONATION: A COMMENTARY

In memory of Heathcote Williams, radical poet and passionate republican

Its terrible fascination is threaded into gold cloth
large gems, amethyst and pearl
we have tried to move with the times
with carefully-chosen faces in all shades
they hold regalia so far removed
from where we are
the abbey flinches

uphold and maintain according to the law
the Law
the Law of Princes
how could it be otherwise?

Technicolour pageantry
is, we are told by a pundit, what the country does best
symbolic order
orders of power, hereditary
gold-braided, gleaming
is that not shameful
given what's outside the mighty doors?

This time the bishops have prompt books
as if words too light for memorizing
might float off
where chorister sincerity wings upward
qui tollis peccata
misere nobis

gowns, staffs, chains of office
rattle as the congregation stands:
do not cease to pray
deliver us from darkness

from benighted shine of gold
visible and invisible
dominion

o clap your hands, ye people
one kind of king or another
send them begone
the book of right honourables
preaches deliverance to the captives
a closed book
the king is on a carpet page

behold a faint shine on vellum
alleluia for that
not for the rest, glossed by servility
the bruised and broken-hearted get passing mentions
privilege nods to duty
it's not enough
what is the natural world, in this temporary

upside-down claim of service
gifts of spirit, freedom
we are opened to love, opines archbishop
stockinged and buckled
the blinking king now unweighted, unfreighted
of ermine
he's not shivering on a scaffold

the naked truth is an accident of birth
supertunica absurdity
does not conceal that
nor how brave advocates for those in need
do not live in palaces
blunted sword of mercy
let me be blunt

girdled with a sword
reform what's amiss
fat chance
elsewhere bombs are falling
more widows and orphans

answer when they call on you
the kingdoms of this world are a mess

before he's gloved in holy power
we glimpse the king has bitten nails
nervous man under a holy coat
please god don't preserve any of this
those who swear their loyalty
have prompt cards
liege men all, so help me god

those with the words before them
recite them in full
they can read
can they not remember words of loyalty
is it so rare these days
and to the queen, brisk business
sceptered, fiddling with her hairdo

righteousness doesn't make things right
the trumpeting of ceremony
does not usher in better
those good things their prayers obtain
they will keep for themselves and their heirs
free of taxes
not weighing our merits

each in our preferred language
our help is in ourselves
put not your trust in princes
think about the tragedy of the commons
and not by the way at all
how the girl choristers were made to have a uniform hairstyle.

COXITATIONS
for Claire Cox, poet

Visiting her surrounds I see
how exact her description is
how a square of light moves, disappears
how those struck by grief, by injury, by illness

cry in pain or shrink into silence
including herself.
Nonetheless she plumes herself
ready for connective crackles

bard of birds, in feather and song
offering them pools of warm love
piper to her dying dog, propped, wiped, fed
stroked, stroked, stroked tenderly

intimates within the tribal flows of newsfeed
we hear the headlines, clockwork of disasters
tangles of puppet strings and puppets
bearable to think about only through artistry.

When she shakes the apple
you hear pips rattle
worm in the bud too
gnawing despair

until a robin hops in at the kitchen door
and she writes of it
in falling apples
truths that we know cannot be healed.

DEATH LIKE LOVE CAN BE AMBIGUOUS

I do not mention your name in my house
or anywhere else

a slab of indifference
is propped between us

wherever molecules of you might have fallen
into cracks have been sandblasted out

white walls fresh painted
with murals of adventures

nonetheless I am tempted
for one night only

to remember you kindly
and wish for your voice.

DESERT FLOWER

Do you not think my secret equal to yours?
Neither of us has said
what we really think

regardless, deepness is
a desert flower
locked up by rain

our light seed's resurrection
hunts for suitability
tumbling across sand.

DISPUTED ELECTION RESULTS

The dictator may go away
may not go quietly
may not go at all
what then?

X in the box, ballot box, boxed in
out on the streets
the dictator's soldiers fire tear gas
water cannon, live bullets

yet another memorial will be installed
carefully away from actual bloodstains

tarmac, cobbles, via dolorosa
paths of glory lead to the grave
isn't that better than the long
bitter roads of conquest?

Let us each have our say
and have our say counted
so the unaccountable are held to account
and dictators wither away.

DULAS BROOK, GOLDEN VALLEY, HEREFORDSHIRE

I

Moon duets with snow
iced glissade

there are tracks in the sky
prints of bear, sheep and lion
through tree-weave owl hoots carry
whoo-who up the valley to the brook plashing behind an old
                                                                                    house

slate, moss, wood
expand their places
expounding mysteries
dew, fog, rain

greens curl in ferns above
the hop-it traces of creatures
jointed, legless, scaled, furred
whose eyes shine in the dark

by day the valley's flooded with silver
fish bones poke up where monks
were laid to unquiet rest
orisons, advowsons, glebe resurface

II

Ripples flow down the road
watery prophecy, watery legend

once dragons lived where now
sheep populate the fields

grass lush and dragon-green
their gates are strung with plainsong minims

by the lane a shuffling pigeon, broken-winged
blinks terrified eyes

she knows who's coming.
In the morning, only tufts

testify. It is an iron world
its trees are shod with fungi

things disappear and reappear
prayers in childbirth, milk from the cow

the last horse plodding round a wooden press
ferments the valley into heady cider.

III

Incumbent reverend wrinkles his nose
at yet another body to be laid in his chancel

miasmas, noxious vapours, will seep
even through a new close-fitting slab

or so he thought. Now beeswax and chrysanthemum
layer devotional air

slant sun turns glass to crimson holy fire
stone pales as bones insist solidity is temporised

we look, admire the monuments and brasses
we read grave names and contemplate

while ghost of reverend sniffing disapproval
hovers in the nave, offended still.

IV

Woodpecker carries blood of Christ on its pate
songthrush tells you when river's in spate
by moving inward

the long dark mountain shoulders its burden
only its own
there's no room for ours

confluence, theological
dottedness of abbey, church and chapel
yews are ecumenical, adopting sanctity

from the porch gate a path winds to graves and church door
the lintel sports a dragon
rampant, clawing at time

cherubs, skulls and angels
stand guard over stony-sad words
the named dead, dates carved and crumbling.

Grief curls in ivy, clinging, fruiting
sorrow in parting is tamed, is wild
whey-pale as the dairymaid

ghosts lie in other counties too
pebbles in brooks, sponged by green flood
but here the ghosts of ghosts gather

reading from folios, spitting in hedges
trudging the land with leaky boots
wayward dogs follow, faithful to heresy

abbot and lord, serf and novice
farmer and ferryman, miller and cook
oak and beech, larch and holly

women, who are lynchpins, know
what a flying buttress is
and what is immoveable bloodstain.

EDEN TREE

The shattered apple
bent double, old dame
broken-backed

as if a grafted knowledge tree
whose fruit was always
there was more to know.

ELEPHANT IN THE ROOM

The cutlery is ivory-handled
seeing ivory, I hope the future asks
what's that?

ELEPHANTINE

Bedrock and sediment, our conversations
skirt round pachyderm
in the rooms where we are
in the rooms we may or may not inhabit.

Looking ahead, what's round corners is
grim. We get there by slow crash.
I'm holding a steering wheel
doubtfully.

We've run out of road.
I've run out of words.

Exhaust fills the rooms
where we are, where we
may or may not inhabit

round elephant corners
holding a steering wheel
disconnected.

EXPLOSIVE

It is dangerous to be female, deathly
it is a crime to speak a foreign language
it is a sin to be you
violence is hunting you

in a country full of soldiers, missiles, minerals
men with guns take over again
old rulers, new rulers
claiming purity and theocratic power

frantic messages, help, please help me
go unanswered
you go to the airport, terrified
where a crowd presses thick and a stinking river
with a four hour crossing stands between you and possible gates
opened

but you do not know the man next to you
wears a suicide vest
and in two minutes' time
both you and he will be smithereens.

FERN

Fern with feathers like quill pen
green ink, air writing

along each frond tilt leaflets
whose awkwardness comes

to be balance, incrementally
pitch perfect

more than anything its simple existence
expresses plant nation

one of many, all for one
rooting together

sermons in ferns, ruffling
both science and revelation

it is a mystery
how I have come to love it so.

FLOOR CLEANER
For my brother Chris.

He writes in such impeccable italic
it might be chronicle or psalm

sloping hand for sloping label
floor cleaner

he also serves who stands and mops
fine action, squeegee

a squirt of soap, scrub, rinse and dry
produces cleaner floor

gleamingly, for whom
celestial promise is reflected
in shine, sun-booted

you pour down drains
the mucky silt
rinse bucket, prop heroic mop
against a door

and walk away
floor cleaner.

FOR NOW THE TREES

I

For now the trees have no headaches
no fumes of diesel, petrol, no soot or grime
for now, briefly, humans are uncentred

giant ash and silver birch
neighbours, guardians, sentinels
play with clouds in unscratched skies

their breathing deep as silence
you can hear leaves breathe
for now the trees have no cough, no overheating

II

Canopy of dappled rustle
shares breaking news
traffic's back

the birch is restless
high up its smallest leaves
sense trouble

for now the humans are stirring
moving, starting up their coughing cars
and trees will have headaches again.

FRAGMENTS OF A HISTORY IN A DREAM
Inspired by RÉVE (Romantic Europe Virtual Exhibition); also published in a special edition, 'Material Romanticism', in Romanticism on the Net (ronjournal.org)

I: PORLOCK VISITATION

The man who wants money
has a leather-bound ledger
his shoes are mud-splashed
in his pockets are ciphers
the sedition of shortfall at our table

come back another day, I say
I am busy
Poetry of eglantine, labyrinthine
wording in serpentine toils
does not want me disturbed

other disturbances call – the nation, the sunset
loose laundry aflap in the hedges
we dine again on barley and turnips
listening for rustles, for rumours
collecting taxes for a coming war.

II: TERESA GUICCIOLI'S TRAVELLING CHEST

In her travelling box are medicaments
against aches, agues, period pains
and miasmas

some people are walking miasmas
after their company, a potion is required
to prevent dissolution of spirits

some people are dissolute
before their company, a powder or two
to fortify liver and heart is desirable

some people are desirable
no powder or pill can provide a solution
so one might as well enjoy it

and to the full
because the fever of this roving life will all too soon
stop, as finally hearts do.

III: THE NOCTOGRAPH

We haven't got to the haptic yet
those still entranced by fountains of lava
look away now

this is about not looking
he went blind in youth
eyes at sea, salt-scarred, fog-seared, infected
promising career cut short

at first he was deterred
then he was not deterred
taken by an urge to travel
he followed it, blindly

seeking out unseeable but highly perceptible places
the other side of the world
and people
horse-scented Tartar whose leathers
held sweat that had foamed in particular patterns

he took a machine to record all this
bandying words on the road
every night through his fingers
he coaxed with tact from wires
his way of being
he could not see the moonlight but he felt it.

IV: IRON

Draped on a sofa the Regency woman
has fiery eyes and shapely feet
tea coffee chocolate
stain her sugar white dress

beside her a candelabra
slender, tall, props a Grecian lamp
nothing is simple
it too has been worked over

wrought iron, cast iron, white iron
folding carriage steps, corkscrews, knives
railings, looms, machines and ships
iron bars to madden the insane

progress makes progress
progress makes efficiency into a superfluity of things
iron signpost with lettering readable at night
shackles and manacles

bilboes, spiked collars
tongue gags, thumbscrews
leg irons, jaw-forcing speculum
branding irons

voyage iron, re-exported
for axes and hoes
treadle and pulley
trade in reverse

but the weight of the chains is iron
like the ironmaster's coffin
and the lock on the door
and the twisted heart topping an elegant candelabra.

V: HEVA

> *A Mourning Dress brought back from Tahiti by Captain James Cook.*
> 'The chief mourner carries in his hand a long flat stick, the edge of which is set with shark's teeth, and in a phrenzy, which his grief is supposed to have inspired, he runs at all he sees, and if any of them happen to be overtaken, he strikes them most unmercifully with this indented cudgel, which cannot fail to wound them in a dangerous manner.' John Hawkesworth, *An Account of the Voyages Undertaken by the Order of His Present Majesty for Making Discoveries in the Southern Hemisphere* (1773)
> 'The head mourner was believed to be inspired by the spirit of the deceased to take revenge on any person who had done him injustice during his lifetime.' Barbara Schaff

Oluuahuuaooolaku
red feather spirit
flies in my body

rage of grief
sways guide-ropes of soul
it beats to be free

red bird sings
the song of our ancestors
against injustice

it falls to me
in feathers
of anger

glimmer of pearl shells protect me
sharpness of shark teeth
arm grief

pearly morning of woe
keen hour of howl
allowable revenge

through a slit of pearl mask I can see
nothing of here
it lets in beyond

whom shall I strike to avenge the injustice
against our dead queen, our people
our green coconut world

every single European
whose foot has disturbed our sand
whose gun has blasted our magic

they who have brought diseases to us
they who trade anger with no outrigger
they who have stolen our sky

oluuahuuaooolaku
the iron-wood tree gives me breath
bark cloth takes our blood.

VI: ADDRESS TO THE SCHOLARS

You search for material remnants of our lives
as if they could speak volumes
or pamphlets at least, hot off a radical press

inked letters spell out forms
to imagine
how the books, the sketches, the offcuts

made travels in our heads
keys to the tomb
bridges, sacrifices

orange, gold, whiteness
satin and stone
neither one nor the other

a pirate's shroud
wrapping in gladness and madness
poetics of things

which outlive us
to repeat and repeal
the purgatory of our expurgation.

HANGING SCROLL

Between Heaven and Earth lies the poetic pool
into which a brush is dipped

heart blossoms
on silk which will last for centuries

I want you to see how
and why I have painted your heart.

HISTORY INSIDE OUT

Subtly week by week the verges change
cow parsley to yarrow to ragwort
succession of thistles in purples and fluff
ox-eye daisies who neither toil nor spin
except in the mind's eye revolving
as the road curves and slopes
into a straggle of trees and new build
presaging a town

fields thick as oils
slabbed, in wheaten shades
hedges nibbled and rolling
protractor straight lines
in furrows and crop stalks

green handkerchiefs have sheep
safely grazing, old money-bags
in sight of the river where monks fished their dinners
and willows toss silver prayers into greenleafed
pools of histories you can't now know

in summer the valley is pastoral
in winter, floodwater drowns half the fields
and the road with a view from above
has verges of silence and a shipful of stories
flowing from elsewhere
obscuring the lovely, the lush, the peaceful valley
of the Windrush.

IMPROMPTU

What does procrastination steal
from time that is expended
on dull routine?

On a day so hot the roads became tar sands
I went with a friend to the river to swim

five cygnets and their parents
bubbled through wreaths of green weed

turquoise darts skimmed by
I swam through cool water, eye level with dragonfly

ragwort and river daisies bordered one bank
swords of iris phalanxed the other

midstream I floated, cloud reflected
curled feather's faint inflection in the water

bathers in the shallows, timeless
mothers and children, laughter, chat

my friend and I happy, startled by the newness
of what we knew well

dry grass our carpet, heat-towelled
cloaked again in clothes

we would have said, why
don't we do this more often

but time, procrastination's thief
laid out the tarry road to dullness
duty-bound.

INTIMATES DOWN UNDER

Having collected the sperm from a captive male koala
a process which involves a rubber vessel
and a human concentrating all his attention on slippery things
and of course a male koala who looks strangely unperturbed –
the human carefully carries his trophy semen
to another room
                where a female koala
arrives from her close-wired enclosure
to be settled in, teased apart, splayed.

While the man transfers semen to a pipette
you need to know that in the wild
koalas mate in trees
she climbs to a high branch, outlier, end-stopped
he calls, a throaty bellow, first from afar
then nearer, louder as he climbs the tree
where she expectantly observes.
They are vertical now, pairing
he bites her neck for grip
but how to stop his semen running out with gravity
down to a useless below?
                        There is a way to get this right.
Forty thrusts eject a goo, a gluey cloud
two more shoot sperm right through this gelling wad
which plugs his offering in.

So we return to lab and man, pipette in hand
fingers hunting for her opening
her gaze is completely unreadable
and he, does he wake at night and think of work
new ways of pleasuring koalas?
He does his best, counting thrusts
twenty-seven, twenty-eight

this helps genetic diversity
thirty-one, thirty-two

at thirty-three she waggles her ears

at forty the man says, last two
done
her gaze is inscrutable.

By way of comparison among marsupials
a male kangaroo, buck twice the size of doe
has balls in front of his penis
which can be let down to cool in a breeze
an echidna digs a hole beside his mate
he sidles in aside to straddle
sideways on, spinelessly
but with a remarkable penis
it has four swivellable heads
like a Remington electric razor
two will fill her branched canal
that's very clever
cleverdick echidna

Why couldn't the cleverdick humans
make the koalas a love pole and let them get on with it
'Basil' and 'Ella', tagged signifiers, figleaves for indignity
this will help genetic diversity for sure
what does it do for species relationships?

IRINYA, KATYA, VERA…

Irinya in headscarf and ripped soul
sobs in her garden
where in the bombsite wreckage
a carpet blooms
under it is her dead son
she dug his grave herself.

Katya has three condoms and a pair of scissors
she was cornered
by four soldiers.

Vera has a picture burnt into her head
young girls, naked, hung from trees.
Her neighbour chopped her daughter's hair
so she'd look like a boy.
That didn't fool the soldiers.

Anna said the war will be over when the tulips bloom
it has not ended
red holes are everywhere.

Marina is terrified for her children
she cannot protect them any more
after weeks in a basement with no water
one bucket
sixteen people
they drained the radiator to make tea
she touched only her lips with brown water
so the kids could have more.

Somewhere in another country said to be safe
a little boy presses his face to a window

longing for his mother
who is on the front line.
He cannot say anything to anyone.
Explosions grow inside his head.

JAMJAR NASTURTIUMS

The nasturtiums are flaming reminders
and in their jamjar thin green stalks
insist that the unsupportable
practically
can burst out in unlikely beauty
intensest orange, deep yellows, dark red

artwise, still life, but more than that
even as their lightweight silk
puckers in decay
their veined throats deepen
as if to say
you can still do this, and in your own way.

KEEP THE ART BOOKS

In my dotage I will sit and drool
over crucifixions
bloody madonnas and saints of pristine holiness
I will think nothing except there they are
suffering

if you say, somewhere in the body
a soul struggles to inhabit then get free
will I believe you
seeing in viscous toils of oil
bodies protesting

suffering the impositions corruptions degradations of flesh
in return for desire
half-wittingly shall I then turn to sunlight
orchards, children's laughter
the tapestried hare?

LEVER BOX

An operant conditioning chamber permits experimenters to study behaviour conditioning by teaching a subject animal to perform certain actions, like pressing a lever, in response to specific stimuli, such as a light or sound signal. When the subject correctly performs the behaviour, the chamber mechanism delivers food or other reward.

Needs may be satisfied
        in unsatisfying ways
                by finding the laws
and obeying them.

Pigeon
        encased
                entombed
no room to turn
        no space to unfold
                pinned wings.

Damn the cramped walls
        electrified floor
                the lack of light
the monsters who thought this thing up.

Hunger
        may be accompanied by wonder
                these scientists are not interested in that
they want results.

Time passes.
        Time stops.
Time crawls into brain and stomach.

Hooklets
> barbules
>> barbs
>>> shafts of every feather

glued together
> by waiting
>> for what it is not clear
yet.

This could go on for ever. Forever. For ever and ever.
Pull the lever, press the switch, peck the black box
whatever it is
holding forever forward, backward.
A pellet drops out.

> Starving gobbles it
>> cries for water
>>> grunts, stamps, sniffs for crumbs.
There are none.

The Law of Obedience offers
Rewards, but at a
Price. And without any
Choice.

In this hell a pigeon can only do the thing its masters demand of it
the only thing, which it can master
quite easily – it's not stupid –
which is to act as they want.

Pigeon or crackpot scientist
whose careers are advanced by hypothesis
which high-flyers are trapped in behavioural boxes?

Drooped, denied the sky
the pigeon's remarkable magnetic compass
rusts away
so does its soft excitable coo.

The masters, apparently satisfied
turn out the lights and leave for home.

MARBLED IN FOAM

You sail in a golden ship over the hilltops
out of a sunrise that grows pearly and greener
like dew in the dawn

your mycelium secret
is openly beautiful and deserving
leaf-fall applause

tight fit at first it becomes tailored
to whatever and whoever you will be
marbled in foam upon the great seas

and your vivacity will swirl, until
cast with design of coccolithophore
recognition sinks, quietly, to

spangles of light, all night
in currents and clouds
dissolving salts in effervesce.

MEDELLIN HIPPOS

'The hippos brought by Pablo Escobar to his private zoo have multiplied and invaded Columbia's waterways.' BBC News (21 February 2021).

They wallow in wetlands where nothing attacks them except
                                                    humans
too aggressive to castrate and too indeterminate to kill
it is said they have rights of persons, under the law
and people fear spirits

too big to catch they are feared
as the drug-running warlord who bought them for show
look on my works, ye puny
gape hippo-like at power

the hippos are happy, very happy
nothing impedes them, there is plenty of food
there are rains, suitable pools
deep greenery they can populate

but without passports they are stateless
and a dangerous precedent.
Delay increases costs for humans –
what should they do about the Medellin hippos?

Lumbering invasive species
displaced in a new niche
they innocently trample over natives
unaware that paradise is human-ruled.

MIMESIS
for Lorine Niedecker, poet

Professors
are key workers
they file serrated edges
observing differences of fit
they also make the locks.

*

Philosophy attends to the particular
russet apple lunch
bites of generality
the golden orchards of Hesperides.

*

Garden quaggy from rain
is thick with self-sown
seedlings for which I am not responsible
push forward
night and day

*

Grain of pine table
good rest for writing wrist
elbows off the table said my mother
what would she say
to poet's prop?

*

Pearl-handled fish forks
no longer obligatory on Fridays
seem prissy, snooty, strange
and beautiful.

MOVING IN
For Katharine

She has her first keys in a purse in a shoulder bag
to unlock a kingdom all her own

playing houses under a sheeted kitchen table
she made up cosiness, child-friendly

now there's a store room that might make a study
a kitchen lurid in pink

which she outgrew, along with spangles and
that dodgy cleavage phase

what does it matter if there's love
and a new double bed

and the keys to her own first home
jingling the dissonance of bills and independence.

MY FRIEND SHIRLEY SAYS SHE WILL PRAY FOR RAINBOW

Up there with the shining ones
she tells me
putting deerhound among the saints
I will pray for him

his breed is polite, even with heart trouble
though of wild appearance
unless brushed and collared
I think he will behave

if the saintliness of saints rubs off
does dog numinosity alter the patina of saints?
And if he's up there with the shining ones
what will her prayers heal, catholically?

The thought that counts, counts
clock ticking
in rosaries to an eternity
shared with our elective saints.

NEW YEAR'S EVE

As we lose loved ones
making the most of our own lives
is counterweight

here are invitations
party streamers, midnight carouse
gala, feast, revelry and spree

a big blank page
is inviting me, other intimate
somewhere else.

NOCTURNAL JASMINE
Cestrum nocturnum

No bat winging across a crescent moon
could love you more
unless a night moth drawn in faster

you forgive absence of mud, humidity, sky expanse
you accept a pot
even with a daily thirst for water

your fragrance, honeyed musk
puts into flowers what you forgo
a need for elsewhere.

NORTH LINCOLNSHIRE

Expressive gesture, wordless
wolds run in a wave behind which
sunset is quickened

nothing breaks
neither hearts nor china nor weather
nor fealty

there's promise so old in it that
nobody now knows what it was
nor what exactions followed

nonetheless, loam turned by harrow
recedes in shining clods
all the length of vast fields

supply chain to the nation
cabbages turnips potatoes
all sorts of greens

where village names are pastoral
poetry rebuilt after plague
new cheeses run abroad

Cropwell Bishop, Colston Bassett, Cote Lindum
Lincolnshire Poacher
an oak memorial, he learned his trade here

in woods dappled by daylight
beech rise either side, holding the wave
red clover cresting the pasture

from where you can see, far ahead
the grey blue line
of the sea.

NOW WE ARE SIXTY

From freckles to age spots
skin does its own thing
so too does memory
a simple I forgot becomes forgetfulness
full of forgetting
forget-me-not

all the honey stored comes back in bees
I remember where the blanks begin.

RAINBOW FADES...

There were gladioli in a vase
which seemed to bloom more purple
the night he died

you can't foretell such things as omens
nor can you find
consoling words

the joys were so much greater than the griefs
best outcome
like a stirring shaking sound above your head

then footfall, staircase-descending patter
silky ears, determined muzzle
pressing the case: our bond, our love.

RAINWATCHING

Old metaphors of clouds, weeping
are really our griefs, leaking
dripping, seeping
set in for the day.

REFLECTION

My era has been profuse and profligate.
These are old words and may go extinct.

REMEMBER THE ALAMO

Remember the Alamo, says the sombre cowboy hero
meaning the men, dead men, the fort, the battle, defeat
valiant flag fluttering in dry wind
the sacrifice, the nation-building moment

so much of that is tainted now
it looks like brutal conquest
killing others of a different skin
to take their land

let's rewind
before the fort there was a stream
and poplar trees
los álamos

soft cottonwoods that clustered
round the chapel that a mission built
linked to the water
and providing shade

the cottonwood's a generous tree
grows fast
not strong
turns dazzling gold in autumn

stands as a meeting place or trail marker
makes good canoes
feeds horses with its bark and shoots
shades all from burning sun

they're still there, around the monument
fluffed with spring seeds
thick downy capsules
that spread white cotton like a quilt

remember the alamo
who sees men come and go
smothering the land with downy seeds
over the dead, the blood, the earth, the living.

REREADING 'THE WALRUS AND THE CARPENTER'

Spat spatter splutter
pitter patter
of tiny oysters
in a sandy bed

whyever did they leave it
to join a walrus and a carpenter
what need had they
for bone or wood?

The salt and pepper condiments
were surely clue enough
what lay beyond was bound to be
violence in light verse

they had no feet to trot back home
under the sea-green wave
they had no views on sealing wax
nor how they should behave

when faced with conversation
on vegetables from land.
Their hosts seemed not quite genial
with something cruel planned

and so it proved
the little queens all gobbled up
their juices sopped, their flesh devoured
the empty shells removed.

SEA SHANTY FOR THE COWS IN A FLOATING FARM, THE NETHERLANDS

Hooray and up she rises
because the tide has turned again
there is a tide in the affairs of cows
just as there is for men

Day or night it's hard to tell
if it's heaven or if it's hell
to live a life defined by swell
is not to live a life lived well.

SHE AND HE

He sheds her like an old skin, one
that began silky, shiny, rippling green
and slowly stiffened, tight around his ribs
grew flaky, itchy, mouldering
greying his sight

She, still rippling green and silky
questions his sight
laments to the grass around her
that itchiness
is not her doing

He casts out all mementoes
traces of her having touched his life
washed off his skin
She keeps as relics near her
the casual gifts he gave

He dreams of being easy in his skin
She dreams of touching, skin to skin
He toys with silky new skin
She reaches out for ease

Healing, unhealing, hurting afresh
She has green skin within.

SKIP

I

Rusted bicycle no saddle busted brakes
in forlornly tigerish orange
roofspars, bashed panels
all in the skip

offcuts of words
one perfect for my purpose
is several layers down, wedged.

II

Chunks of cement old plasterboard
bricks bags of sand stubborn plants
all in the skip

offcuts of wood
one perfect for my purpose
is wedged, several layers down.

SLOW-WORM

There are poems in praise of glow-worms
but none that I know of
for the slow-worm

let this be one
eulogy of unrimmed eel-grey smoothness
coiled in a compost heap
basking, looped in curly dreams

by rights they should be emblems of the primitive
ultimately unimaginative in form
and yet articulate reminder
simplicity repeats, repeats, repeats
it is easy to confuse it with a slow-worm.

THE EEL QUESTION

'...the eel is incapable of keeping a diary from which we could draw conclusions regarding its sex.' Sigmund Freud.

Dear Diary
today I feel an urge
to converge
with my kind

a surge of ocean
ripples through me
salt-stiffening

Dear Diary
today I felt prickles of grass
slither under me
it is time to emerge

leave the meadow
head to sea
to finish being me

Dear Diary
I see a garland of eels
diverge and submerge

gliding in the dark
anatomical enigma
does not trouble me.

THE POET'S DOG'S COMPLAINT

This puppy is growing up and knows her place, mostly sofa
her long legs sprawly, sometimes upside down
airing opinions with dignity and grace

she has a role
poet's dog
torch handed on, part of our happy deal
her long straw life

there is no ceremony to install
no surplice, swinging censer, serenading choir
no need for that
only patience

as yet again her afternoon excursion
is deferred
while poet
furrowed brow and narrowed eyes

tries to nail a phrase
in which temporarily
all the universe is concentrated
except for poet's dog.

THE RIVER AT PORT MEADOW
The Thames, upper reaches

Speckles and dapples as the river flows
through summer morning to evening
in minnow time of little fish schools
exploring clear edges of shore
where nibbles of nothings
sustain them whether flickering on
ascatter or resting in the greening shadows of weeds

the river is
the river is a little different every day
like you are
the river is

unstoppable
killable
like you are

each of its curves is singular
yellow flag iris in this one, where dragonflies
are drawn to feed and sport and mate
in this one, reeds slant beacons for grayling
who lie cooling farther out
where silvers merge and float

here where cows gather on hot days
the sandy shore bends into companionability
in whisper of poplars, drift of lime
steady glide of swan

the river ripples and tells you
the river is with you

here where a patch of mud and cowpat
make loam swifts dip for
and scoop all on the wing to carry off
to plaster nest

here where a secret presence is
kingfisher
and a heron openly wily
makes stockstill his stony art form

here, where an old holm oak and a shattered hazel
drink just enough to stay in leaf

the swimmers, winter pink
leave towels on trees whose sap
is river-dappled, whose breathing
is river air and water

picnickers, birders, narrowboats and pleasure craft
kayaks, canoes, single-handed sails
sculls and dinghies
people who speckle and dapple the river

in spring flotilla, wavy, geese teach goslings
unsteadily afloat
how to read the river
to know it, love it, respect and trust it

in speckles and dapples the river holds the last
of light it carries, shares till dark
when starlit current
carries on like time
all flowing to the sea.

THINKING OF ALFRED COHEN
Interior with Important Painting, 1987

Whirlwind reds or pooling depths of blue
having seen both, poppy and aconite
I am torn away from metaphysics
to an interior of chintz
there are poppies again
cool sense of warm lives
hearth, cushions, window
the words have been emptied away
to restore to things the things they can say
furniture solid, indoor life
in flowered print and pot plant
unperturbable logic of greens.

TIME SCALES

I wonder what time scales the makers of the windows of
                                         Chartres thought in
especially when they began
did they know the building would take thirty years
or did they think after ten
O God, the project's over-run

did they think their God would understand
about being late
would He know they had worked their hardest,
their longest into the cold nights
of the Loire valley

or did they think, no need to rush
beauty takes all the time it needs
chipping away, annealing,
piss in the paint pot to thin it
tapping the lead, fractionally, for months

matching up ruby, sapphire, yellow, green
and purple glass
let us not forget the significance of clear
drawing where the light fell
at different times of year
why not

finding the right charcoal for furnace
the right team to raise, carry, finesse
shapes into place
all among the builders
clearing away old stone, uncleanly

what they thought was hammered into colour
scarlet, cobalt, emerald
infusing light into interiority
astonishing the abbot who exclaimed
this church shines wondrously, celestially,
and it was worth the wait.

TODAY

I kicked a mouldering rabbit corpse into the hedge
magpie had pecked at it
kite had stripped it
spaniel had mouthed it
whippet had slavered it, carried it
part-way home

bones and black flesh, furred
a loose-linked creation
skeletal, mortal, rural
countryside casualty
life span
        attention span.

TRIBUTE
In memoriam Paul McLoughlin, poet

Gravelly voice and glittering eye
accosting
his words sandpapered
his jazz haunting jaunty
with unjaunty thought
in case you thought it was safe
or how you believed
cracked true

husking, busking, speaking up
for a child hiding under the stairs
knowing what fear was and fearing knowing
his banter thus barter
or as he'd say
why can't you say what you mean?

WAS IT BETTER THAN SUBURBIA?

I grew up in several climates
temperate hot humid dry
jungle and desert

pyramids and peaks
put triangular
into floating dimension

loosely tethered
they never quite came down

some coalesced
some sank
some punctured

it is only by travelling
that you hear of promised lands

it may be only by residing
that you find them.

WATLINGTON

On a grey summer day we found
a field of pale gold
edged purple with knapweed
and ox-eye daisies
kingdom of butterflies
and hills stretching away

the bridleway has ancient beeches
mystery fungi in delicate black caps
cathedral and playground, wild space
hemmed in by barbed wire

and a notice on the car
when we got back
Do not park on this land.

WAYFARER

If he stank to high heaven
he was at least spiritually ahead
of those who'd shy away

like me
from this encounter
on a random side street

as he caressed my dog
his warm and grimy touch
said neither take it nor leave it but give it

I wondered how the dog knew
he was heavenly –
in both of them, sagacity and trust.

WISHBONE

Having roasted two chickens which cooled
raising the hopes of a deerhound, one eye open, in case
I strip them, greasy job
noting anatomy
wings are puny these days
breast so overweighted
I go back to a childhood kitchen
where after Sunday lunches we would
dig out and dry the wishbone
take turns in pulling it

occasional winner, what did I wish for?
I can't remember
a wish granted in winning the bigger part
it wasn't a wish for wealth: we managed
we're not poor, joked my mother
we just don't have any money
it was a good lesson in the seriousness of poverty
and in labels: get rid of them.